Learniappe: 111 Creative Ways to us
Copyright© 2012 Learniappe, LLC
All Rights Reserved

MW00465160

$16.95 USA
ISBN-13:
978-1475067286

ISBN-10:
1475067283

Author: Larry Straining, CPLP
Graphics: Mindi Zachary Talley @ www.MTdesignZ.com

All rights reserved®. Copyright © 2012 by Learniappe, LLC. This book may not be reproduced without the expressed written consent of the author.

For discounts on quantity orders of the book contact:
Learniappe Publishing 1-225-266-0599

PRINTED IN THE UNITED STATES OF AMERICA
First Edition

The Fine Print:

We Learn Something Extra© by building on experiences, tools, techniques and theories.

The purpose of this publication is for inspiration and general information. In the spirit of mutual respect, please do not distribute, modify, or revise large chunks of the contents without written permission of the author.

Learniappe, LLC or affliated parties will not be held liable for any damage or loss arising from reading this publication or the use of information to be found on its pages.

Acknowledgements

I have been fortunate enough to be surrounded by people who have supported me my entire life. I have also had the opportunity to have had people who have told me I can't do something. To those who said I can't, thank you! Can't is a huge motivator for me. To those who have supported me, I am blessed to have had you in my life and am extremely grateful for you.

I am extremely grateful to *Kimberly Seeger* for seeing merit in my idea and allowing me to add something extra to the *Learniappe...111* series of books. Also for providing the time and support in guiding me in this project.

I am so appreciative of the additional support from *Renie McClay* for reviewing my work and looking over my virtual shoulder throughout the process. And to *Mindi Talley* who took the images from my head and put them together as a gorgeous book cover.

Most importantly I want to say how much I appreciate my wife *Cindi* and daughter *Kyrielle* for picking up the slack during the times I sequestered myself from them during this process.

Who is this book for?

Well, as cliché as it may sound, it is for everyone.

Are you new to using QR Codes? This book will help show you the diversity of the technology.

Are you experienced with using QR Codes? This book will help get you thinking of other areas that use QR Codes.

How could you use this book?

This is a book to read when you are stumped, or creatively stagnant. Flip through the book at random or focus on an area outside your normal field. Don't let the categories box in your creativity, but use them as a spark to get you thinking of new ways you can use QR Codes.

When reading this book I encourage you to take notes. When you think of something new, write it down immediately so it is not lost.

Table of Contents

What is a QR Code?

QR (Quick Reference) Codes are the remarkable 2D codes that link the real world to the virtual world. They are used in just about every industry and are extremely versatile. Easy to create, QR Codes can include phone numbers, text messages and hyperlinks to any number of materials on the internet.

How can I read a QR Code?

To read (use) QR Codes you need an application on a mobile device, such as a smart phone or tablet, with a camera and an internet accessible web browser. Your distance from the code and the quality of your camera can impact your experience. There are many applications that are stand-alone QR Code readers as well as applications that include reading QR Codes as a secondary function. I suggest that you go to your device's application store and do a search for QR Code readers. You will discover quite a few, so download several of them to try until you find the one you like the best.

How can I test a QR Code?

For users who will be creating QR Codes I suggest that you download as many readers as you can find. As a QR Code creator and user, I make sure I test all of my codes on many readers and from multiple distances and angles. I do not want to exclude any end users.

Where do I start?

There are many services and ways, both paid and free, to create QR Codes. For the sake of simplicity I am going to include my favorite site for creating the codes. I could probably include 111 ways to create QR Codes, but that is a different book. http://qrcode.kaywa.com/ is the site I use the most. It is a free site that accepts donations for its ongoing development.

Creating a QR Code is extremely simple using this QR Code Generator.

First, select whether you want the QR Code to contain a URL, Text, Phone Number, or SMS.

Selecting a URL will link your QR Code to content on a web site, this can be a web page, a video, a document or other downloadable file.

Selecting Text will allow you to enter a text message 250 characters long that will display on the screen of the person scanning the QR Code.

Selecting the Phone Number option allows you to enter a phone number that will display on the screen of the person scanning the QR Code.

Selecting SMS allows you to set up a number and a message that can be sent from the device of the person scanning the QR Code.

Next, enter your content. This field will change based on which type of QR Code you selected. Finally, click the <u>Generate</u> Button.

Your QR Code will appear in the display area on the left side of the application.

When you right click on the QR Code graphic you just created you have the option save it as a graphic file or you may cut / copy and paste it into a document.

Materials

QR Codes are generated using a computer program. Once they are created, however, the pattern can be recreated using any number of materials.

1) Building blocks

2) Colored papers

3) Icing

4) Cloth

5) People

6) Needlepoint

7) Whiteboards

8) Candies

9) Buttons

10) Computer graphics

What other creative materials can be used to create QR Codes?

_____

_____

_____

_____

Locations

QR Codes can be displayed on any number of surfaces.

11) Clothing

12) Food

13) Jewelry

14) Temporary Tattoos

15) Products

16) Posters

17) Books

18) Kiosks

19) Trade shows

20) Bulletin boards

What creative locations can you place QR Codes?

_____

_____

_____

_____

rofessional

The professional category includes ideas for QR Codes in business. Large corporations, non-profits, small businesses and entrepreneurs can benefit from incorporation of QR Codes to engage customers and employees.

21) Add a QR Code to link contact info to a business card.

22) Add a QR Code to your luggage for identification.

23) Add a QR Code to all your promotional materials linking to your web site.

24) Include QR Codes on your assembly instructions to link to a video of someone assembling the product.

25) Use a QR Code to collect employee suggestions electronically.

26) Add a QR Code to your receipts to collect customer feedback.

27) Place a QR Code on equipment that requires special instructions.

28) Provide a QR Code that links to videos of special events held at your location.

29) Post internal job openings via QR Code.

30) As a craftsperson you can provide QR Codes linking to finished projects.

31) Place a QR Code on boxes of archived files for storage, listing its contents.

32) Provide QR Codes that link people to your social media sites.

How can you use QR Codes to promote your business?

_____

_____

_____

Video

QR Codes are popular ways of linking to videos; this section focuses on how to use QR Codes within the videos themselves.

33) At the end of a video clip add a QR Code that takes viewers to a web site for more information.

34) When breaking up videos into smaller segments, include a QR Code at the end of one segment that takes you to the next video in the series.

35) During a video add a QR Code that allows viewers to download a document that will be covered in the next section of the video.

36) Add a QR Code to your videos that include a link to the script for ADA regulations.

How can you add QR Codes to your videos in a creative way?

_____

_____

_____

_____

Personal

In the personal category consider how you can use QR Codes around the house and in your personal life.

37) When packing boxes for moving or storage, add a QR Code with the contents of the box.

38) List emergency household numbers in a QR Code.

39) Add a QR Code to your first aid kit linking videos showing emergency first aid procedures.

40) Instead of publicly posting your child's name on coats or backpacks, use a QR Code for identification.

41) Add QR Codes to household appliances that require seasonal maintenance linked to a video of how to prepare the appliance for the new season. (i.e. lighting a pilot light, removing and storing a pool cover.)

42) Add a QR Code to your pet's collar.

43) Place QR Codes in photo albums linking to family videos.

44) Include QR Codes in your scrapbooks linking videos of the events in the book.

45) Add a QR Code to your equipment with contact information for recovery purposes.

How can you creatively use QR Codes to help you personally?

_____

_____

_____

_____

Training

QR Codes in training are a great way to interact with your participants and engage them using technology and tools they are already using on a daily basis.

46) Use as an activity opener, (ice breaker), scan people to find common interests.

47) Use QR Codes to take participants directly to Level 1 Evaluations.

48) Use a sheet of QR Codes that link to your activities, have participants scan the appropriate code when it is time to complete that task or activity during your session.

49) Use a QR Code to link to materials participants will need for each section of training.

50) Provide QR Code links to videos for review after your session is over for performance support.

51) Add a QR Code to your promotional documents that link to videos of participants providing feedback from your sessions.

52) Assume not everyone is going to have a smart phone, use QR Codes as an opportunity to form teams. Each team could have at least one person with a technology enabled device. It can also introduce people to new technology.

What creative ways can you use QR Codes to engage with your participants?

_____

_____

_____

_____

resentations

Similar to Training, using QR Codes in presentations allows you to interact with your participants and engage them using technology and tools they are already using on a daily basis.

53) Add links to the presenter's contact pages at the beginning and end of a presentation.

54) When citing statistics or other reference material, add a QR Code that takes participants directly to the source article.

55) Include a QR Code in your slide decks that allow participants to download your presentation.

56) Use a QR Code to take participants to a survey during a presentation.

57) Add a QR Code to your one-sheets that provides a video of you promoting your session.

58) Place a QR Code on your speaking proposals with a link to a sample video of you presenting.

What creative ways can you use QR Codes to engage with your participants?

_____

_____

_____

_____

Waiting rooms

With lots of down time, waiting rooms are a great place to provide creative activities for people to explore using QR Codes.

59) Include a QR Code with games or puzzles to pass the time.

60) In a doctor or dentist office, add a QR Code with health tips.

61) In a repair shop, provide maintenance tips in a QR Code.

62) Highlight your employee of the month or an exceptional customer.

63) Show video testimonials of your customer service.

64) Use a QR Code to link to new products or services that you will soon be offering.

65) Include a QR Code linking to information about the history of your organization.

66) Add a QR Code linking customers to a survey asking them to rate the quality of service they received.

What creative ways can you develop to use QR Codes in waiting rooms?

_____

_____

_____

_____

Restaurants

Restaurants are just as much about the experience as they are about the food. QR Codes can be a way to creatively engage patrons while they are at your establishment.

67) Have a QR Code on your door that links to your menu.

68) Run a QR Code special for an appetizer or a dessert.

69) Highlight your exceptional chef or server of the month.

70) Include a video of some signature dishes being prepared.

71) Create a video showing how to execute a particular cooking technique.

72) Highlight upcoming live acts.

73) Provide recipes for common dishes.

74) Provide holiday meal tips.

75) Provide etiquette tips.

76) Use a QR Code to drive people to a customer service survey.

What creative ways can you use QR Codes in restaurants?

_____

_____

_____

_____

Marketing

Marketing is about promotion. Hey, look at me! Hey, look at my product! Using a QR Code in your marketing can draw people to your product as well as provide that follow up step of engagement when your QR Codes are scanned.

77) On food products include a QR Code that links to recipes using that product.

78) Run contests accessible via a special site linked to a QR Code.

79) Link to video testimonials of people using your product.

80) Lay out your products in a pattern to form a QR Code that can be scanned.

81) Provide do-it-yourself tips on your products using a QR Code.

82) Use a QR Code to suggest other products that complement this product.

83) Add a QR Code to your sport team's uniform linking to the player's statistics, making them a living sports card.

What creative ways will you use QR Codes to market yourself and your products?

_____

_____

_____

_____

Disguises

This category isn't about dressing up as a QR Code but provides ways of including QR Codes in other designs, in effect disguising the QR Code.

84) Incorporate your logo into the QR Code itself.

85) Incorporate a QR Code into your logo.

86) Use a site such as GlassGiant.com to spice up your graphics by making them part of a larger graphic.

87) Color code your QR Codes for different departments or content areas.

What can you do to creatively disguise your QR Codes?

_____

_____

_____

_____

Conferences

Conferences of any size deal with people and information. This area focuses on how the two things can easily be linked together.

88) Add contact information to a participant's name badge.

89) Add a link to important conference information on the back of participants' name badges, such as schedules or maps.

90) As participants enter a breakout session have a QR Code that downloads the documents for the session.

91) Provide a list of local restaurants and include a QR Code that provides a map to get to each location.

92) Post QR Codes showing some simple exercises or stretches people can do while at a long conference.

93) Have staff wear a QR Code with FAQs during events.

94) Post QR Codes to show videos of highlights of recent conferences held at a location.

95) In your programs, for each session, include a QR Code that takes participants to a video of the presenter promoting their session with key takeaways.

What creative ways can QR Codes make your next conference experience more interactive?

_____

_____

_____

_____

Museums

Museums, national parks and galleries are each full of items for people to enjoy and experience. Linking a QR Code to the items provides a way for the audience to engage further with the experience.

96) Display a QR Code at registration that links to a map of the building.

97) Place a QR Code next to each exhibit telling more about the artist or the piece itself.

98) Provide QR Codes linking videos highlighting groups that have recently toured your facility.

99) Display QR Codes as works of art. (I personally find the patterns of QR Codes very relaxing.)

What creative ways can QR Codes make your next museum experience more interactive?

Schools

We spend a lot of time in schools and build some great memories while there. QR Codes can allow us to connect with those memories in a much more interactive way.

100) Place QR Codes in year books that link to videos of special events, dances or athletic activities.

101) Use QR Codes on student IDs.

102) Create a QR Code scavenger hunt.

103) Post QR Codes in random (unexpected) locations with trivia or jokes.

104) Highlight art or class projects in a QR Code.

105) Use a QR Code to highlight a video of the student of the month getting recognized.

106) Use QR Codes to highlight videos of exceptional sports moments in a trophy case.

How can you use QR Codes in a creative way in your school?

_____

_____

_____

_____

Authors

Using QR Codes, authors can now interact in creative ways with their readers.

107) Place a QR Code on your contact page taking readers to more information about you.

108) Use QR Codes in your book that takes readers to videos showing processes or how to execute tasks.

109) Use a QR Code to take readers to a web site with more of your works.

110) Include a QR Code that takes readers to a web site where they can learn where you will be speaking on the topic of your book.

111) Add a QR Code that links to your blog for continued conversations about your book topic.

How can you use QR Codes to creatively interact with your readers?

_____

_____

_____

_____

Keep it Simple!

A lot of information in your QR Code itself, such as a long URL, can make for a complicated or busy QR Code.

Let me suggest that when you create a QR Code that you use a program called a link shortener in order to make the link smaller and unclutter the QR Code. I am a fan of a website called bitly.com.

Notice the difference in the previous two QR codes. Both codes will work, both codes take you to the exact same web site (the site for this book). However, the second one is less cluttered and can be used in some tighter locations. In addition, by using bitly.com I am provided with some valuable analytics, partially shown below.

Join the Discussion

You have just scanned 111 Creative Ways to use QR Codes in a variety of areas with the purpose of sparking your creativity. What creative new ways have you discovered in which you can use the technology?

If you are involved with School events, how can you use ideas from Marketing or Waiting Rooms? If you are a Trainer, what ideas from Museums can you use to help engage your participants? Explore, experiment and experience how you can creatively use QR Codes in different areas of your world.

Let's continue the discussion. When you come up with something new, scan the QR Code on the front of this book. The QR Code goes to a web page for ongoing discussion. I encourage you to share your ideas that may appear in 111 MORE Creative Ways to use QR Codes.

Record Extra Learning Notes:

_____

_____

_____

_____

_____

_____

_____

What steps will you take to be more engaging using QR Codes?

_____

_____

_____

_____

_____

_____

About Learniappe

Learn a little Something Extra!

Learniappe is a solutions-focused advisory and support firm with extensive experience and enigmatic passion for continued learning. Learniappe was inspired by the French term, Lagniappe, which means to receive more or an extra benefit.

Learniappe occurs when we learn something extra and add to our knowledge, skills and experiences.

To order additional copies of this publication or explore other learning opportunities, please visit: www.learniappe.com

eNews: Learniappe distributes periodic electronic newsletters distributed by email subscription. Input your email address (respectfully never released to third parties) to receive ideas, tools and techniques to design and facilitate learning.

Subscribe at www.learniappe.com .

Learniappe Publishing
2012

LEARN iappe

About the Author

Larry Straining, CPLP is a Workplace Learning and Performance professional with over 15 years in the industry. In 2009 Larry founded Larry's Training, LLC, focusing on helping people achieve their goals using creative and innovative technologies.

Larry can be found speaking to organizations across the country on technology related topics. Popular requests include:

- Immersion Learning Strategies
- Learning Technology with Today's Tech Tools
- Social Media boot camps
- SolutionPeople's Accelerate to Innovate workshops.

Larry invites you to connect:

Larry Straining, CPLP
918-809-2670
larry@larrystraining.com

Twitter http://twitter.com/larrystraining
LinkedIn http://www.linkedin.com/in/larrystraining
Facebook http://www.facebook.com/larrystraining
Website & Blog http://www.larrystraining.com

33358966R00029

Made in the USA
San Bernardino, CA
30 April 2016